Web Development 101: Building Websites from Scratch

The book covers the following:

Chapter 1: Introduction to Web Development

1.1 Understanding the Basics of Web Development

1.2 Essential Web Development Languages: HTML, CSS, JavaScript

1.3 Overview of Web Development Tools and Technologies

1.4 Setting Up a Development Environment

1.5 Web Development Best Practices and Standards

6.3 Designing for Screen Readers and Assistive Technologies

6.4 Keyboard Accessibility and Focus Management

6.5 Testing and Auditing Web Accessibility

Chapter 7: Server-Side Programming

7.1 Introduction to Server-Side Programming Languages

7.2 Setting Up a Server Environment (e.g., Node.js, PHP)

7.3 Handling Form Submissions and Data Processing

7.4 Working with Databases (e.g., MySQL, MongoDB)

7.5 Server-Side Frameworks and APIs

Chapter 8: Database Integration

8.1 Introduction to Relational and Non-Relational Databases

8.2 Structuring and Designing Database Schemas

8.3 Querying and Manipulating Data with SQL

8.4 Database Security and User Authentication

8.5 Integrating Databases into Web Applications

Chapter 9: Content Management Systems (CMS)

9.1 Introduction to Content Management Systems

9.2 Exploring Popular CMS Platforms (e.g., WordPress, Drupal)

9.3 Installing and Customizing CMS Themes

9.4 Managing Content and Media in a CMS

9.5 Extending Functionality with Plugins and Modules

Chapter 10: Web Performance Optimization

10.1 Importance of Web Performance and Page Speed

10.2 Optimizing CSS and JavaScript Files

10.3 Minification and Compression Techniques

10.4 Caching and Content Delivery Networks (CDNs)

10.5 Performance Testing and Optimization Tools

Chapter 11: Web Security and Best Practices

11.1 Understanding Common Web Security Threats

11.2 Securing Websites with HTTPS and SSL Certificates

11.3 Handling User Input and Form Validation

11.4 Protecting Against Cross-Site Scripting (XSS) and SQL Injection

11.5 User Authentication and Authorization

Chapter 12: Deploying and Maintaining Websites

12.1 Deploying Websites to a Web Server

12.2 Domain Registration and DNS Configuration

12.3 Website Backup and Version Control

12.4 Monitoring and Performance Tracking

12.5 Continuous Learning and Professional Development

Chapter 1: Introduction to Web Development

Web development can be divided into three parts: client-side coding, server-side coding, and database technology. Client-side coding refers to the code that runs on the user's computer, in their web browser. This code is responsible for the look and feel of the website, and for interactivity such as forms and animations. Server-side coding refers to the code that runs on the web server. This code is responsible for the functionality of the website, such as processing form submissions and connecting to databases. Database technology refers to the database software that stores the data for the website. This can be a relational database such as MySQL, or a NoSQL database such as MongoDB.

Web development can be further divided into two parts: front-end development and back-end development. Front-end development refers to the client-side coding, and back-end development refers to the server-side coding. Front-end developers are responsible for the look and feel of the website, and for creating interactive features such as forms and animations. Back-end developers are responsible for the functionality of the website, such as processing form submissions and connecting to databases.

The first step in web development is to choose a domain name and web hosting. Domain names are the unique addresses of websites on the internet, and web hosting is the service that provides the technology and space for websites on the internet. Once you have chosen a domain name and web hosting, you can begin coding your website.

There are many different programming languages that can be used for web development, but the most popular ones are HTML, CSS, and JavaScript. HTML is used to structure the content of a website, CSS is used to style the look of a website, and JavaScript is used to create interactive features on a website.

After you have created your website, you will need to publish it on the internet. This can be done by uploading your website files to your web server. Once your website is live, anyone in the world will be able to access it by typing your domain name into their web browser.

1.1 Understanding the Basics of Web Development

Web development is the process of creating and maintaining a website. It includes everything from adding new features to fixing bugs. Web developers use a variety of programming languages and tools to create a website.

The basics of web development include understanding how the web works, how to write code, and how to use HTML, CSS, and JavaScript to create a website.

1.2 Essential Web Development Languages: HTML, CSS, JavaScript

The three essential web development languages are HTML, CSS, and JavaScript. HTML is used to create the structure of a web page, CSS is used to style the content of a web page, and JavaScript is used to add interactivity to a web page.

1.3 Overview of Web Development Tools and Technologies

There are a wide variety of web development tools and technologies available today. Some of the most popular include:

- HTML and CSS: These are the basic building blocks of any website or web application. HTML is used to structure content, while CSS is used to style it.

- JavaScript: JavaScript is a programming language that is used to add interactivity to websites and web applications.

- PHP: PHP is a programming language that is often used in conjunction with HTML and CSS to develop dynamic websites and web applications.

- MySQL: MySQL is a database management system that is often used in conjunction with PHP to store data for dynamic websites and web applications.

- Apache: Apache is a web server software that is used to host websites and web applications.

- Linux: Linux is a open source operating system that is often used to run web servers.

1.4 Setting Up a Development Environment

There are many different ways to set up a development environment, and the best way depends on your needs. If you just need a basic environment to write and run code, you can use a text editor and a simple command-line interface. If you need a more complex environment for developing large applications, you can use an Integrated Development Environment (IDE).

A text editor is a program that allows you to write and edit code. There are many different text editors available, and the best one for you depends on your preferences. Some popular text editors include Sublime Text, Atom, and Visual Studio Code.

A command-line interface (CLI) is a way to interact with a computer by typing commands into a text interface. The CLI is often used for running programs or scripts, and for accessing system settings. Many operating systems come with a built-in CLI, and there are also many third-party CLIs available.

An IDE is a software application that provides a comprehensive development environment for software development. IDEs typically include a text editor, a compiler or interpreter, a debugger, and other tools. Some popular IDEs include Microsoft Visual Studio, Eclipse, and Xcode.

1.5 Web Development Best Practices and Standards

There is no definitive answer to this question as best practices and standards vary depending on the specific context of web development. However, some general tips that may be useful for web developers include:

- Keeping code clean and well organized
- Using comments to document code
- Using consistent coding conventions
- Testing code regularly

- following accessibility guidelines
- optimizing code for performance
- using a version control system

Chapter 2: HTML Fundamentals

2.1 Introduction to HTML: Structure and Syntax

HTML is the standard markup language for creating web pages and web applications. With HTML you can create your own website.

HTML is easy to learn - You will enjoy it!

HTML is a markup language

A markup language is a set of markup tags

HTML uses markup tags to describe web pages

HTML documents are described by HTML tags

Each HTML tag describes different document content

HTML tags are usually called HTML elements

HTML elements are the building blocks of HTML pages

HTML documents are structured into HTML elements

HTML elements can contain other HTML elements

HTML documents are text files with HTML tags

HTML documents are read by web browsers

HTML documents can be written with any text editor

A web browser reads HTML documents and displays them as web pages.

The HTML syntax is the set of rules that define how an HTML document can be written.

HTML documents must start with a document type declaration: <!DOCTYPE html>.

The document type declaration tells the web browser about the version of HTML used in the document.

HTML documents must start with a <html> tag.

The <html> tag tells the web browser that this is an HTML document.

HTML documents must have a <head> element.

The <head> element contains information about the document, such as the document's title, author, and keywords.

HTML documents must have a <body> element.

The <body> element contains the document's content, such as text, images, and links.

HTML elements are written with start tags and end tags.

The start tag is written with a less-than sign (<) and the end tag is written with a greater-than sign (>).

HTML tags are not case sensitive.

HTML documents must be well-formed.

A well-formed HTML document must have matching start and end tags for all HTML elements.

2.2 HTML Elements and Tags

HTML elements are the building blocks of HTML pages. They are used to create structure and format content.

HTML tags are the labels that tell browsers how to display HTML elements. They are enclosed in angle brackets (< and >).

Most HTML elements have an opening tag and a closing tag. The closing tag has the same name as the opening tag, but with a forward slash (/) before the tag name.

For example, the opening tag for a paragraph element is <p>, and the closing tag is </p>.

Some HTML elements do not have a closing tag, such as the br element (which represents a line break). These elements are known as empty elements.

The content of an HTML element is everything between the opening and closing tags. For example, the content of the paragraph element above is "This is a paragraph."

Attributes are used to provide additional information about HTML elements. They are added to the opening tag of an element, and are usually made up of a name and a value.

For example, the href attribute is used to specify the URL of a link. The value of the href attribute is the URL that the link should point to.

<a href="http://www.example.com">This is a link</a>

In the example above, the value of the href attribute is "http://www.example.com". This value is the URL that the link will take the user to when clicked.

Attributes can be used to specify the values of HTML elements. For example, the value of the alt attribute can be used to specify the text that should be displayed if an image can't be displayed.

```
<img src="logo.png" alt="Company Logo">
```

In the example above, the value of the alt attribute is "Company Logo". This value will be displayed if the image can't be displayed.

2.3 Creating Headings, Paragraphs, and Text Formatting in HTML

Headings are created with the h1 to h6 tags. Paragraphs are created with the p tag. Text formatting can be done with the strong, em, and u tags.

2.4 Working with Links and Images in HTML

When working with links and images in HTML, it is important to understand how the HTML code is structured. In HTML, there are three main elements that are used to create links and images: the anchor element, the image element, and the link element.

The anchor element is used to create a link to another web page. The anchor element has two attributes: href and target. The href attribute specifies the URL of the page that the link will go to. The target attribute specifies where the linked page will be opened. The target attribute can have one of three values: _blank, _self, or _parent.

The image element is used to insert an image into an HTML document. The image element has two attributes: src and alt. The src attribute specifies the URL of the image. The alt attribute specifies an alternate text for the image.

The link element is used to create a link to another web page. The link element has two attributes: href and rel. The href attribute specifies the URL of the page that the link will go to. The rel attribute specifies the relationship between the current page and the linked page.

2.5 Building Forms and Input Validation in HTML

Forms are one of the most important components of any web application. They allow users to input data, which can then be processed by the application. Forms can be used to login users, register new accounts, place orders, and much more.

HTML provides a number of elements that can be used to build forms. The most important form element is the <form> element. This element defines the boundaries of the form and contains all the other form elements.

Other important form elements include:

<input> - used to input data

<select> - used to create drop-down menus

<textarea> - used to input large amounts of text

<button> - used to submit the form

Input Validation

Once a user has inputted data into a form, it is important to validate that data before processing it. Invalid data can cause errors in the application or allow malicious users to exploit the application.

HTML5 includes a number of new attributes that can be used to validate input data. These attributes include:

required - specifies that an input field is required

pattern - specifies a regular expression that an input field must match

min/max - specifies the minimum and maximum value that an input field can have

step - specifies the increment that an input field can have

These attributes can be used to ensure that data is entered in the correct format and within the correct range.

Chapter 3: CSS Styling

3.1 Introduction to CSS: Selectors and Properties

CSS selectors are used to select the element or elements you want to style. There are a variety of CSS selectors available, and you can even create your own.

CSS properties are the attributes of an element that you can change. For example, you can change the color, font, size, and position of an element. There are a variety of CSS properties available, and you can even create your own.

3.2 Applying Styles to HTML Elements

When it comes to applying styles to HTML elements, there are three main ways to do so: inline, internal, and external.

Inline styles are applied directly to the HTML element that you want to style. This is done by adding the style attribute to the element, and then specifying the CSS rules that you want to apply to that element.

Internal styles are added to the head section of an HTML document. This is done by using the <style> element, and then specifying the CSS rules that you want to apply to the document.

External styles are added to an external CSS file, and then that CSS file is linked to the HTML document. This is done by using the <link> element, and then specifying the URL of the CSS file.

When it comes to deciding which method to use, it really depends on the situation. In general, inline styles are best for small changes, internal styles are best for larger changes that affect the whole document, and external styles are best for changes that affect multiple documents.

3.3 Working with Colors, Backgrounds, and Borders using CSS Styling

When it comes to CSS styling, colors, backgrounds, and borders are all important aspects to consider. Colors can be used to set the tone of a website, and can be used to highlight important information. Backgrounds can be used to add visual interest, and can be used to create a sense of depth. Borders can be used to frame content, and can be used to create a sense of separation.

When working with colors, it is important to consider both the foreground and background colors. The foreground color is the color of the text, and the background color is the color of the area behind the text. It is important to choose colors that will be easy to read, and that will not clash with the other colors on the page.

When working with backgrounds, it is important to consider the size, shape, and color of the background. Backgrounds can be used to add visual interest, and can be used to create a sense of depth. Backgrounds can also be used to frame content, and can be used to create a sense of separation.

When working with borders, it is important to consider the width, style, and color of the border. Borders can be used to frame content, and can be used to create a sense of separation. Borders can also be used to highlight important information.

3.4 Layout and Positioning Techniques using CSS Styling

CSS provides various properties to control the layout and positioning of elements on a web page. The position property can be used to position elements relative to the document, or relative to another element. The float property can be used to floated elements to the left or right of the containing element, and the clear property can be used to prevent elements from floating next to each other.

The z-index property can be used to control the stacking order of elements, and the overflow property can be used to control how elements are clipped or scroll when they are too large for the containing element.

CSS also provides properties to control the spacing between elements, such as the margin and padding properties. The box-sizing property can be used to control how the width and height of elements are calculated.

In addition to the standard CSS properties, there are also various CSS3 properties that can be used to control the layout and positioning of elements. The flexbox and grid properties can be used to create flexible and responsive layouts. The transform and transition properties can be used to create animations and transitions.

3.5 Responsive Design and Media Queries using CSS Styling

Responsive design is a web design approach that aims to provide an optimal viewing experience—easy reading and navigation with a minimum of resizing, panning, and scrolling—across a wide range of devices, from desktop computer monitors to mobile phones.

Media queries is a CSS technique introduced in the CSS3 specification that uses media types to conditionally apply styles. A media query consists of a media type and at least one expression that limits the style sheets' scope by using media features, such as width, height, and color. Media queries, added in CSS3, let the content be tailored to a specific range of output devices without having to change the content itself.

Example:

@media only screen and (max-width: 600px) {

```css
body {

background-color: lightblue;

}

}
```

Chapter 4: JavaScript Basics

4.1 Introduction to JavaScript: Functions and Variables

A function is a set of instructions that can be run over and over again. A function can take input, called arguments, and produce output. Functions can be written into JavaScript code or stored in separate files called libraries.

A variable is a named value that can be changed within a program. In JavaScript, variables can be declared using the var keyword. Once a variable is declared, it can be assigned a value. The value of a variable can be changed throughout the program.

4.2 JavaScript Data Types and Operators

In JavaScript, there are six primary data types: strings, numbers, Booleans, objects, functions, and undefined. In addition, there are two composite data types: arrays (which are ordered lists of values) and regular expressions (which are patterns used to match strings).

JavaScript also has a number of operators that can be used to manipulate values. The most basic operators are the assignment operators, which are used to assign values to variables. The assignment operators are: =, +=, -=, *=, /=, and %=.

The arithmetic operators are used to perform mathematical operations on numbers. The arithmetic operators are: +, -, *, /, and %.

The comparison operators are used to compare two values. The comparison operators are: ==, !=, ===, !==, >, <, >=, and <=.

The logical operators are used to combine two Boolean values. The logical operators are: && (AND), || (OR), and ! (NOT).

The bitwise operators are used to perform operations on the individual bits that make up a number. The bitwise operators are: & (AND), | (OR), ^ (XOR), ~ (NOT), << (left shift), >> (right shift), and >>> (zero-fill right shift).

The typeof operator is used to determine the data type of a value. The typeof operator is written as: typeof x, where x is the value whose data type is being determined.

The delete operator is used to delete a property from an object. The delete operator is written as: delete x, where x is the property to be deleted.

The in operator is used to determine whether a property exists in an object. The in operator is written as: x in obj, where x is the property to be checked and obj is the object.

The instanceof operator is used to determine whether a value is an instance of a particular type. The instanceof operator is written as: x instanceof Type, where x is the value to be checked and Type is the type to be checked for.

4.3 Controlling Program Flow with Conditional Statements and Loops in JavaScript

In JavaScript, there are several ways to control the flow of a program. The most common way is to use conditional statements, which allow you to execute a certain block of code only if a certain condition is met. For example, you might want to execute a certain piece of code only if the user is logged in, or only if the user is over the age of 18.

Another way to control the flow of a program is to use loops. Loops allow you to execute a certain block of code multiple times. For example, you might want to execute a certain piece of code 10 times, or 100 times.

There are two main types of loops in JavaScript: for loops and while loops. For loops are best suited for situations where you know exactly how many times you want to execute a certain piece of code. While loops, on the other hand, are best suited for situations where you want to execute a certain piece of code an unknown number of times.

Finally, there is also the break keyword, which allows you to break out of a loop prematurely. This can be useful if, for example, you want to stop executing a certain piece of code after the user has made a certain number of mistakes.

In summary, there are several ways to control the flow of a program in JavaScript. The most common way is to use conditional statements, which allow you to execute a certain block of code only if a certain condition is met. Another way to control the flow of a program is to use loops, which allow you to execute a certain block of code multiple times.

4.4 DOM Manipulation and Event Handling in JavaScript

DOM Manipulation and Event Handling are two very important concepts in JavaScript. DOM

Manipulation refers to the process of changing the structure, content, or style of a web page using JavaScript. Event Handling refers to the process of responding to events that occur on a web page, such as when a user clicks a button or link.

Both DOM Manipulation and Event Handling are essential for creating interactive web pages. DOM Manipulation is used to change the appearance of a web page, and Event Handling is used to respond to user input.

DOM Manipulation

DOM Manipulation is the process of changing the structure, content, or style of a web page using JavaScript. The Document Object Model (DOM) is a tree-like representation of a web page. It is used by web browsers to interpret and display web pages.

JavaScript can be used to change the structure of a web page by adding, removing, or modifying elements. It can also be used to change the content of an element, or to change the style of an element.

Event Handling

Event Handling is the process of responding to events that occur on a web page, such as when a user clicks a button or link. Events are actions that can be detected by a web page.

JavaScript can be used to respond to events. When an event occurs, a function can be executed. The function can perform any actions that are desired, such as displaying a message, or redirecting the user to another page.

DOM Manipulation and Event Handling are essential for creating interactive web pages. They are used to change the appearance of a web page, and to respond to user input.

4.5 JavaScript Libraries and Frameworks

There are many different JavaScript libraries and frameworks available for developers to use. Some of the most popular include jQuery, AngularJS, ReactJS, and Node.JS. Each of these libraries and frameworks provides different functionality and features, so it is important to choose the one that is best suited for the project you are working on.

jQuery is a JavaScript library that makes it easy to access and manipulate HTML elements. It also provides a number of other features, such as event handling, animation, and Ajax support.

AngularJS is a JavaScript framework that lets you create single-page applications. It uses a Model-View-Controller (MVC) architecture, which makes it easy to organize your code. AngularJS also provides two-way data binding, which means that changes to the model are automatically reflected in the view.

ReactJS is a JavaScript library for building user interfaces. It uses a declarative programming model, which makes it easy to create complex UIs. ReactJS also has a virtual DOM, which makes it fast and efficient.

Node.JS is a JavaScript runtime that lets you run JavaScript code on the server. It also provides a number of features, such as a package manager and an event-driven programming model.

Chapter 5: Responsive Web Design

5.1 Understanding Responsive Web Design Principles

Responsive web design (RWD) is a web design approach that provides an optimal viewing and interaction experience across a wide range of devices, from desktop computer monitors to mobile phones. RWD is based on a "fluid grid" system, which is a series of rows and columns that expand and contract as the screen size changes. The content within the grid also adjusts itself automatically, so that it is never too small or too large for the viewer.

RWD is not just a matter of making a website look good on all devices; it is also about making it easy for users to interact with and navigate the site, regardless of the device they are using. In order to achieve this, RWD uses a combination of flexible layouts, images, and cascading style sheets (CSS).

The first step in creating a responsive web design is to create a fluid grid. This is done by setting up a series of rows and columns, and then using CSS to make them expand and contract as the screen size changes. The content within the grid also needs to be responsive, so that it is never too small or too large for the viewer.

The next step is to use media queries to determine the width of the device being used. Media queries are a CSS3 feature that allows different stylesheets to be applied depending on the width of the device. This is how RWD is able to adjust the layout of a website to the width of the device.

Once the width of the device is known, the layout can be adjusted to fit. This may involve changing the width of the columns, the size of the images, or the amount of text on the page. The goal is to make the website easy to read and navigate, regardless of the device being used.

RWD is not just about making a website look good on all devices; it is also about making it easy for users to interact with and navigate the site, regardless of the device they are using. In order to achieve this, RWD uses a combination of flexible layouts, images, and cascading style sheets (CSS).

5.2 Creating Flexible Layouts with CSS Grid and Flexbox

Flexible layouts are essential to responsive web design. CSS Grid and Flexbox are two powerful tools that can be used to create flexible layouts.

CSS Grid is a two-dimensional layout system that can be used to create responsive layouts. It is composed of rows and columns, and each element can be placed in a specific row and column. CSS Grid is very powerful and can be used to create a wide variety of layouts.

Flexbox is a one-dimensional layout system. It is composed of flex items, which can be laid out in a row or column. Flexbox is very powerful and can be used to create a wide variety of layouts.

Both CSS Grid and Flexbox are essential to responsive web design. They can be used to create a wide variety of layouts that are responsive to the viewport size.

5.3 Media Queries for Responsive Styling in Responsive Web Design

Media queries are a powerful tool for creating responsive designs. With media queries, you can create different stylesheets for different screen sizes. This means that your design can adapt to different screen sizes, making it more responsive.

Media queries are based on the @media rule, which allows you to specify different styles for different media types. For example, you could use a media query to create a different stylesheet for print media, or for screen media.

Media queries can be used to target specific screen sizes, orientations, and resolutions. This makes them very powerful for creating responsive designs.

There are a few different ways to write media queries. The most common way is to use the @media rule, which is supported by all major browsers.

Another way to write media queries is to use the @import rule. This method is not supported by all browsers, but it is supported by most major browsers.

Finally, you can use media queries directly in your CSS. This method is not supported by all browsers, but it is supported by most major browsers.

Here is an example of a media query using the @media rule:

```
@media screen and (max-width: 480px) {

/* styles for screens that are 480px or less go here */

}
```

This media query will target screens that have a width of 480px or less. The styles inside the media query will only be applied to screens that match this criteria.

Here is an example of a media query using the @import rule:

```
@import url("styles.css") only screen and (max-width: 480px);
```

This media query will target screens that have a width of 480px or less. The stylesheet will only be loaded on screens that match this criteria.

Here is an example of a media query using a CSS rule:

@media only screen and (max-width: 480px) {

/* styles for screens that are 480px or less go here */

}

This media query will target screens that have a width of 480px or less. The styles inside the media query will only be applied to screens that match this criteria.

5.4 Responsive Images and Media in Responsive Web Design

The term "responsive images" refers to images that can be scaled to fit different screen sizes. In responsive web design, responsive images and media are an important part of creating a responsive website.

Responsive images can be created in a number of ways, including using the srcset attribute, using the picture element, or using CSS media queries.

The srcset attribute allows you to specify different images for different screen sizes. The picture element allows you to specify different images for different screen sizes and pixel densities. CSS media queries allow you to specify different styles for different screen sizes.

When using responsive images, it's important to consider the file size of the images you are using. Large images can slow down your website, so it's important to use images that are the right size for the screen they will be displayed on.

There are a number of tools that can help you optimize your images for different screen sizes, including the ImageOptim tool and the Cloudinary service.

In conclusion, responsive images and media are an important part of responsive web design. There are a number of different ways to create responsive images, and it's important to consider the file size of the images you use. There are a number of tools that can help you optimize your images for different screen sizes.

5.5 Testing and Debugging Responsive Websites

When testing and debugging responsive websites, it is important to test across a variety of devices and screen sizes. This will ensure that the website looks and functions correctly on all devices.

There are a few different ways to test responsive websites. One way is to use a responsive design testing tool such as Adobe Edge Inspect or Google Chrome Developer Tools. These tools allow you to view the website on different devices and screen sizes and test how it looks and functions.

Another way to test responsive websites is to simply use a mobile device or tablet to view the website. This will give you a good idea of how the website looks and functions on a smaller screen.

Finally, it is also important to test the website on a desktop computer. This will ensure that the website looks and functions correctly on larger screens.

Testing and debugging responsive websites can be a bit tricky. However, by using a variety of devices and screen sizes, you can ensure that the website looks and functions correctly on all devices.

Chapter 6: Web Accessibility

6.1 Understanding Web Accessibility Standards and Guidelines

There are a number of web accessibility standards and guidelines that aim to make the web more accessible for people with disabilities. These include the Web Content Accessibility Guidelines (WCAG) 2.0, the Accessible Rich Internet Applications (ARIA) 1.0, and the United States Access Board's Section 508 Standards.

The WCAG 2.0 are a set of guidelines developed by the World Wide Web Consortium (W3C) that aim to make web content more accessible to people with disabilities. The guidelines are organized around four principles: perceivable, operable, understandable, and robust.

The ARIA 1.0 is a set of guidelines developed by the W3C that aim to make web applications more accessible to people with disabilities. The guidelines are organized around four principles: perceivable, operable, understandable, and robust.

The Section 508 Standards are a set of guidelines developed by the United States Access Board that aim to make electronic and information technology more accessible to people with disabilities. The standards are organized around four sections: 1194.22 Web-based intranet and internet information and applications, 1194.23 Desktop and portable computers, 1194.24 Telecommunications products, and 1194.25 Video and multimedia products.

6.2 Semantic HTML and Proper Document Structure

Semantic HTML is HTML that introduces meaning to the web page rather than just presenting content. Semantic HTML is important for accessibility because it allows screen readers to interpret the page more easily and it makes the page more understandable for people with cognitive disabilities.

Proper document structure is also important for accessibility. A well-structured document is easier to navigate and understand. Proper document structure also makes it easier for screen readers to interpret the page.

6.3 Designing for Screen Readers and Assistive Technologies

Screen readers are software programs that allow blind or visually impaired users to read text on a computer screen. Assistive technologies are devices or software programs that help people with disabilities use computers and other devices.

There are a few things to keep in mind when designing for screen readers and assistive technologies:

1. Make sure that all text is accessible to screen readers. This includes text in images, buttons, and form fields.

2. Use clear and simple language. Screen readers can have difficulty with complex sentence structures.

3. Use descriptive link text. Screen readers will read the link text aloud, so make sure it accurately describes the destination of the link.

4. Use headings and labels to organize content. Screen readers allow users to navigate content by headings and labels, so make sure they are clear and descriptive.

5. Use alternative text for images. Screen readers will read the alternative text aloud, so make sure it accurately describes the image.

6. Use captions and transcripts for videos. Screen readers can't read video content, so captions and transcripts are essential for making videos accessible.

7. Use data tables wisely. Screen readers can have difficulty with complex data tables. If possible, use simple tables or use row and column headers to make the data more accessible.

8. Test your design with a screen reader. The best way to find out if your design is accessible is to test it with a screen reader.

6.4 Keyboard Accessibility and Focus Management

Keyboard accessibility is the ability to use a keyboard to interact with a website or web application. This includes the ability to navigate to different parts of the page, select different elements on the page, and enter information into forms.

Focus management is the ability to control where the focus is on a page. This is important for keyboard accessibility because it allows users to navigate the page without having to use a mouse.

There are a few different ways to make a website or web application keyboard accessible. The first is to use the tab key to move the focus around the page. This can be used to move between different elements, such as links, form fields, and buttons.

The second way to make a website or web application keyboard accessible is to use shortcut keys. Shortcut keys are a combination of keys that can be pressed to perform a certain action. For example, the shortcut key for the home page on most websites is Alt+Home.

The third way to make a website or web application keyboard accessible is to use ARIA roles. ARIA roles are attributes that can be added to HTML elements to give them a certain meaning. For example, the role of "button" can be added to a link to make it clear that it can be clicked.

There are a few different ways to make a website or web application focusable. The first is to use the tabindex attribute. The tabindex attribute can be added to any HTML element to make it focusable. For example, the following code would make a link focusable:

```
<a href="#" tabindex="0">Click me!</a>
```

The second way to make a website or web application focusable is to use the autofocus attribute. The autofocus attribute can be added to any HTML element to make it automatically receive focus when the page is loaded. For example, the following code would make a form field automatically receive focus when the page is loaded:

```
<input type="text" autofocus>
```

The third way to make a website or web application focusable is to use JavaScript. JavaScript can be used to set the focus to any element on the page. For example, the following code would make a link receive focus when the user clicks on it:

```
<a href="#" onclick="this.focus();">Click me!</a>
```

Keyboard accessibility and focus management are important for making websites and web applications accessible to all users. By using the techniques described above, you can make your website or web application accessible to users who use a keyboard, as well as those who use a mouse.

When testing and auditing web accessibility, there are a few key areas to focus on:

1. Content accessibility: Is the content on the website accessible to all users, including those with disabilities? This includes checking for things like alternative text for images, closed captioning for videos, and transcripts for audio content.

2. Navigation accessibility: Can users navigate the website using only a keyboard, or other assistive technologies? This includes making sure that all links and form controls are properly labeled and that the website's structure is easy to understand.

3. Functional accessibility: Do all the website's features work properly with assistive technologies? This includes things like testing how well screen readers work with the website's content and checking for any issues with using a keyboard to navigate the site.

4. Aesthetics accessibility: Is the website's design accessible to all users, regardless of their visual impairments? This includes checking for things like sufficient color contrast and avoiding the use of flashing or blinking content.

Testing and auditing web accessibility can be a time-consuming process, but it's important to ensure that your website is accessible to all users. By following the guidelines above, you can help make sure that your website is accessible to everyone.

Chapter 7: Server-Side Programming

7.1 Inthroduction to Server-Side Programming Languages

Server-side programming languages are used to create web applications. A web application is a collection of web pages that interact with a user. The web pages are stored on a web server and the user accesses them through a web browser.

Web applications are usually written in a server-side programming language, such as PHP, ASP.NET, or Java. The code in a server-side programming language is executed on the web server, and the results are sent to the web browser.

Server-side programming languages are also used to create web services. A web service is a collection of web pages that can be accessed by a program. The web pages are stored on a web server and the program accesses them through a web service interface.

Web services are usually written in a server-side programming language, such as PHP, ASP.NET, or Java. The code in a server-side programming language is executed on the web server, and the results are sent to the program.

7.2 Setting Up a Server Environment (e.g., Node.js, PHP)

Assuming you have a server-side programming environment set up, there are a few things you need to do in order to set up a server environment for your web application.

First, you need to make sure that your web server is able to process the programming language you are using. For example, if you are using PHP, you need to make sure that your web server has the PHP module installed.

Next, you need to configure your web server to use the correct file extension for your programming language. For example, if you are using PHP, you need to configure your web server to use the .php extension for files that contain PHP code.

Finally, you need to make sure that your web server is able to execute the code in your files. For example, if you are using PHP, you need to make sure that your web server has the PHP interpreter installed.

7.3 Handling Form Submissions and Data Processing using Server-Side Programming

When a user submits a form, the data is sent to the server for processing. The server can then do something with the data, such as save it to a database, or use it to generate a response to the user.

Server-side programming languages, such as PHP, Ruby on Rails, and ASP.NET, provide a way to write code that runs on the server and can interact with the form data. This code can be used to process the data in some way, such as saving it to a database, or generating a response to the user.

When the server receives the form data, it will first need to parse it and then store it in a data structure, such as an array or object. The server-side code can then loop through the data and do something with each piece of information, such as saving it to a database or generating a response.

Some server-side programming languages, such as PHP, provide functions that can be used to process form data. For example, the PHP function $_POST can be used to retrieve form data that has been sent via the POST method.

Once the server has processed the form data, it can then generate a response to the user. This response can be in the form of a HTML page, or it can be a JSON or XML response that can be used by a web application.

7.4 Working with Databases (e.g., MySQL, MongoDB)

Databases are used to store data in a structured format. They can be used to store data in a variety of formats, including text, numbers, images, and so on. Databases can be used to store data in a variety of formats, including text, numbers, images, and so on. Databases can be used to store data in a variety of formats, including text, numbers, images, and so on.

MySQL is a popular database management system. It is used to store data in a relational format. MongoDB is a popular document-oriented database management system. It is used to store data in a JSON-like format.

Both MySQL and MongoDB can be used with PHP. PHP has built-in functions for interacting with both MySQL and MongoDB.

7.5 Server-Side Frameworks and APIs

In computer programming, a server-side framework is a software framework that is designed to support the development of dynamic websites, Web applications and Web services. The most popular server-side frameworks are ASP.NET, JavaServer Pages (JSP), PHP and Ruby on Rails.

A server-side framework provides a structure for the web pages and web applications that run on a web server. It includes a set of libraries and tools that allow developers to create dynamic, interactive web applications. A server-side framework is typically used in conjunction with a client-side framework, such as AngularJS or React, to provide a complete web application development platform.

The main purpose of a server-side framework is to abstract away the details of the underlying web server and provide a consistent programming interface for developing web applications. This allows developers to focus on the business logic of their applications, without having to worry about the details of the web server.

A server-side framework typically includes a set of APIs that provide access to the underlying web server functionality. These APIs allow developers to create web pages and web applications that can be dynamically generated based on user input.

In addition to the APIs, a server-side framework typically includes a template engine that can be used to generate the HTML for the web pages. The template engine allows developers to separate the presentation layer of their applications from the business logic.

A server-side framework is typically used in conjunction with a database, such as MySQL, to store the data for the web application. The database can be used to store the data for the user session, as well as the data for the application itself.

The benefits of using a server-side framework include the following:

1. It provides a consistent programming interface for developing web applications.

2. It abstracts away the details of the underlying web server.

3. It includes a set of libraries and tools that allow developers to create dynamic, interactive web applications.

4. It can be used in conjunction with a template engine to generate the HTML for the web pages.

5. It can be used in conjunction with a database to store the data for the web application.

Chapter 8: Database Integration in Web Development

8.1 Introduction to Relational and Non-Relational Databases

A database is a collection of data that can be accessed by computers. There are two main types of databases: relational and non-relational.

Relational databases are organized into tables of data, with each table containing multiple rows and columns. Tables are linked together by relationships, which allow for data to be queried and retrieved from multiple tables. Relational databases are typically used for applications that require complex data analysis, such as financial analysis or customer relationship management.

Non-relational databases, also known as NoSQL databases, are not organized into tables. Instead, data is stored in a format that can be easily queried and retrieved. NoSQL databases are typically used for applications that require high performance, such as real-time data analysis or social media applications.

8.2 Structuring and Designing Database Schemas

When designing database schemas, it is important to consider how the data will be used and accessed. For example, if data is going to be accessed frequently, it is important to design the schema so that data can be retrieved quickly and easily. Additionally, if data is going to be updated frequently, it is important to design the schema so that it can be easily updated without impacting other parts of the schema.

When designing database schemas, it is also important to consider the relationships between different pieces of data. For example, if data is going to be related to other data in the database, it is important to design the schema so that these relationships can be easily represented and queried. Additionally, if data is going to be shared between different parts of the database, it is important to design the schema so that data can be easily and accurately shared.

8.3 Querying and Manipulating Data with SQL

SQL, or Structured Query Language, is a powerful language for querying and manipulating data in a database. In web development, SQL is often used to retrieve data from a database and display it on a web page.

SQL can be used to select specific data from a database, update data in a database, or delete data from a database. SQL can also be used to create new databases and tables.

To use SQL in a web development project, a web developer will need to have access to a database server. Most web hosting providers offer database servers that can be used for development projects. Once a web developer has access to a database server, they can use any number of database management tools to write and execute SQL queries.

One of the most popular database management tools is phpMyAdmin. phpMyAdmin is a free, open source tool that can be used to manage MySQL databases. phpMyAdmin can be used to write and execute SQL queries, as well as to manage database users and permissions.

Another popular database management tool is Microsoft SQL Server Management Studio. SQL Server Management Studio is a tool that can be used to manage Microsoft SQL Server databases. SQL Server Management Studio can be used to write and execute SQL queries, as well as to manage database users and permissions.

Once a web developer has a database management tool, they can begin writing SQL queries. SQL queries are written in a specific syntax that must be followed in order for the query to be executed correctly.

The syntax for a SQL query can be divided into four parts: the SELECT statement, the FROM statement, the WHERE statement, and the ORDER BY statement.

The SELECT statement is used to specify which columns from a database table should be returned in the results of a query.

The FROM statement is used to specify which database table should be queried.

The WHERE statement is used to specify which rows from a database table should be included in the results of a query. The WHERE statement can be used to specify criteria that must be met in order for a row to be included in the results.

The ORDER BY statement is used to specify the order in which the rows from a database table should be returned in the results of a query.

Once a SQL query has been written, it can be executed against a database. The results of a SQL query can be displayed on a web page, or they can be stored in a variable for use in other parts of a web application.

8.4 Database Security and User Authentication

Database security is a critical component of web development. User authentication is a key part of database security. User authentication is the process of verifying the identity of a user. There are many ways to do this, but the most common is to use a username and password.

When a user attempts to log in to a website, the website will check the username and password against a database of registered users. If the username and password match a record in the database, the user is considered authenticated and will be granted access to the website. If the username and password do not match any record in the database, the user is considered not authenticated and will be denied access to the website.

Database security is important because it helps to protect the data that is stored in the database. If a database is not secure, it is possible for unauthorized users to access the data. This can lead to the loss or theft of sensitive information. It can also lead to the corruption of data.

User authentication is important because it helps to ensure that only authorized users can access the website. This helps to protect the website from unauthorized access. It also helps to ensure that only authorized users can access the data that is stored in the database.

8.5 Integrating Databases into Web Applications

When building a web application, it's important to consider how the various components will work together. In particular, the web application will need to interact with a database in order to store and retrieve data. There are a few different ways to integrate a database into a web application.

One approach is to use a server-side scripting language (such as PHP, Ruby on Rails, or ASP.NET) to directly interact with the database. This approach is simple and easy to implement, but it can be less efficient because each time a web page is requested, the server has to execute the code to retrieve the data from the database.

Another approach is to use an application server (such as JBoss, WebLogic, or Tomcat) that provides a middle layer between the web application and the database. The application server can handle tasks such as connection pooling (which helps to improve performance by reusing database connections) and caching (which stores data in memory so that it can be retrieved more quickly). This approach requires more infrastructure, but it can improve performance.

A third approach is to use a web service to interface with the database. This approach is more complex, but it can offer some advantages in terms of scalability and flexibility.

No matter which approach you choose, it's important to consider how the database will be integrated into the overall architecture of the web application.

Chapter 9: Content Management Systems (CMS)

9.1 Introduction to Content Management Systems

A content management system (CMS) is a system used to manage the content of a website. It is typically used to create and manage digital content, such as text, images, videos, and other files. A CMS may also provide tools for managing the website itself, such as creating and managing users, roles, and permissions.

The term "content management system" is often used interchangeably with "web content management system" (WCMS). While all CMSs can be used to manage web content, not all CMSs are WCMSs. A WCMS typically includes additional functionality for managing the website itself, such as the ability to create and manage users, roles, and permissions.

There are many different types of CMSs available, ranging from simple, self-contained systems to complex, enterprise-level systems. Some CMSs are open source, while others are proprietary. Some are designed for specific types of websites, such as ecommerce websites, while others are more general purpose.

Choosing the right CMS for a website is a critical decision. The CMS should be chosen based on the specific needs of the website and the skills of the website team. A CMS that is too simple may not provide the functionality needed, while a CMS that is too complex may be difficult to use and maintain.

9.2 Exploring Popular CMS Platforms (e.g., WordPress, Drupal)

CMS platforms like WordPress and Drupal offer a great way to manage and publish content. They provide an easy-to-use interface that makes it simple to add and update content. These platforms also offer a variety of features and plugins that can be used to extend the functionality of the site.

One of the great things about using a CMS platform is that it can help to keep your site organized and structured. This can make it easier for visitors to find the information they are looking for. Additionally, CMS platforms can help to automate some of the tasks associated with maintaining a website, such as generating RSS feeds or creating sitemaps.

If you are considering using a CMS platform for your website, it is important to choose one that is right for your needs. WordPress and Drupal are two of the most popular CMS platforms available. Each has its own strengths and weaknesses, so it is important to evaluate your needs before making a decision.

9.3 Installing and Customizing CMS Themes

A content management system (CMS) is a software application or set of related programs that are used to create and manage digital content. CMS themes are templates that determine the look and feel of a website or application that is powered by a CMS.

Most CMS platforms come with a default theme that can be used as-is or customized to better suit the needs of the site or application. In some cases, third-party themes can be purchased or downloaded for use with a particular CMS.

When customizing a CMS theme, it is important to consider the overall design and layout of the site or application. The colors, fonts, and other visual elements should all be chosen carefully to create a cohesive and professional look. The content that will be displayed on the site should also be taken into account when selecting or customizing a theme.

It is also important to make sure that the theme is compatible with the CMS platform and any plugins or extensions that will be used. Otherwise, the site or application may not function properly.

Once a CMS theme has been selected or customized, it can be installed on the server and activated for use. The process for doing this will vary depending on the CMS platform being used.

After the theme has been installed and activated, the site or application can be launched and made available to users.

9.4 Managing Content and Media in a CMS

In a CMS, content and media are managed through a central interface. This makes it easy for users to add, edit, and delete content and media files.

Users can also easily search for content and media files. The CMS can also be used to generate reports on content and media usage.

9.5 Extending CMS Functionality with Plugins and Modules

A plugin is a piece of software that can be added to a CMS to extend its functionality. A module is a collection of plugins that work together to provide a specific functionality.

Adding plugins and modules to a CMS can be a great way to extend its functionality and add new features. However, it is important to be careful when adding new plugins and modules, as they can also introduce new security risks. Make sure to only add plugins and modules from trusted sources, and always test them on a development or staging server before adding them to a production server.

Chapter 10: Web Performance Optimization

10.1 Importance of Web Performance and Page Speed

Web performance is important for a variety of reasons. First, faster web pages lead to happier users. Studies have shown that users are more likely to abandon a slow loading website in favor of a faster one. In addition, faster web pages can lead to higher conversion rates and lower bounce rates.

Second, faster web pages can improve your search engine rankings. Google has stated that page speed is a factor in their ranking algorithm. In addition, faster web pages can lead to higher click-through rates from organic search results.

Third, faster web pages can improve your bottom line. Faster pages can lead to higher conversion rates, which can translate into more sales and more revenue. In addition, faster web pages can lead to lower hosting and bandwidth costs.

Fourth, faster web pages can improve the user experience. Faster pages can lead to a smoother user experience, which can improve the overall satisfaction with your website. In addition, faster web pages can lead to lower abandonment rates and higher retention rates.

Finally, faster web pages can improve the overall health of the internet. By making the web faster, we can reduce the amount of bandwidth that is used and improve the overall efficiency of the internet.

In conclusion, web performance is important for a variety of reasons. Faster web pages can lead to happier users, higher search engine rankings, improved bottom lines, and a better user experience. In addition, faster web pages can improve the overall health of the internet.

10.2 Optimizing CSS and JavaScript Files

CSS and JavaScript files can be optimized to improve web performance. CSS files can be minified and compressed to reduce their size, and JavaScript files can be minified and compressed as well. Additionally, both CSS and JavaScript files can be cached to improve performance.

10.3 Minification and Compression Techniques for Web Performance Optimization

In order to improve the performance of a website, it is important to reduce the size of the files that are being transferred. This can be done by minifying the code, which is the process of removing unnecessary characters from the code, such as whitespace, comments, and unnecessary code. Minifying the code can reduce the file size by up to 70%.

Another way to reduce the file size is to compress the files. This can be done using gzip, which is a tool that compresses files. Gzip can reduce the file size by up to 90%.

Both minification and compression can help to improve the performance of a website by reducing the amount of time it takes to transfer the files.

10.4 Caching and Content Delivery Networks (CDNs) for Web Performance Optimization

One way to improve the performance of a web site is to use a content delivery network (CDN). A CDN is a system of distributed servers that deliver content to a user based on the user's geographic location. The content is delivered from a server that is closest to the user, which reduces the amount of time that the user has to wait for the content to load.

Another way to improve the performance of a web site is to use caching. Caching is a technique that stores frequently accessed data in a temporary storage location so that it can be quickly retrieved when needed. Caching can improve the performance of a web site by reducing the amount of time that is needed to retrieve data from the server.

10.5 Performance Testing and Optimization Tools for Web Performance Optimization

There are a number of performance testing and optimization tools available for web performance optimization. Some of these tools are listed below:

1. Google PageSpeed Insights: This tool analyzes the content of a web page and provides suggestions on how to improve its performance.

2. WebPageTest: This tool allows you to test the performance of a web page in different browsers and on different devices.

3. GTmetrix: This tool analyzes a web page and provides suggestions on how to improve its performance.

4. Pingdom: This tool allows you to test the response time of a web page.

5. YSlow: This tool analyzes a web page and provides suggestions on how to improve its performance.

6. PageSpeed Insights: This tool analyzes the content of a web page and provides suggestions on how to improve its performance.

7. WebPagetest: This tool allows you to test the performance of a web page in different browsers and on different devices.

8. PageSpeed Insights: This tool analyzes the content of a web page and provides suggestions on how to improve its performance.

9. Google Analytics: This tool allows you to track the performance of your website.

10. Google Webmaster Tools: This tool allows you to track the performance of your website and provides suggestions on how to improve its ranking in search results.

Chapter 11: Web Security and Best Practices

11.1 Understanding Common Web Security Threats

Web security threats can come from a variety of sources, including malicious hackers, viruses, and even legitimate websites that have been compromised. The most common web security threats include:

1. SQL Injection: This attack occurs when a hacker inserts malicious code into a website's database, which can then be used to extract sensitive information or even take control of the entire site.

2. Cross-Site Scripting (XSS): This type of attack occurs when a hacker injects malicious code into a web page, which is then executed by the browser of anyone who visits the page. This can be used to steal sensitive information or redirect visitors to malicious websites.

3. Malware: Malware is any type of malicious software, which can include viruses, Trojans, and spyware. Malware can be used to steal sensitive information, damage your computer, or even take control of your entire system.

4. Phishing: Phishing is a type of social engineering attack where a hacker attempts to trick you into revealing sensitive information, such as your username and password, by masquerading as a trustworthy entity.

5. Denial of Service (DoS): A denial of service attack occurs when a hacker prevents legitimate users from accessing a website or service by flooding it with traffic or requests. This can be used to take a website offline or make it unavailable.

6. Man-in-the-Middle (MitM): This type of attack occurs when a hacker intercepts communication between two parties, such as a website and a user, in order to eavesdrop or even modify the data being exchanged.

7. Session Hijacking: This attack occurs when a hacker takes over an active session, such as a user's login session, in order to gain access to sensitive information or perform unauthorized actions.

8. Password Attacks: There are a variety of password attacks, such as brute force and dictionary attacks, which can be used to guess or crack passwords.

9. DNS Spoofing: This type of attack occurs when a hacker modifies the DNS records of a website, which can be used to redirect visitors to a malicious website or even take the website offline.

10. clickjacking: This type of attack occurs when a hacker tricks a user into clicking on a malicious link or button, which can be used to perform unauthorized actions or steal sensitive information.

11.2 Securing Websites with HTTPS and SSL Certificates

HTTPS is a protocol that encrypts and decrypts information sent between a web server and a web browser. This ensures that any sensitive information, such as credit card numbers or login credentials, is not intercepted by third-parties. SSL certificates are used to create a secure connection between a web server and a web browser. These certificates are issued by a Certificate Authority (CA), and they contain information about the organization that owns the website, as well as the website's domain name. When a web browser connects to a website that is using HTTPS, the browser will check the SSL certificate to make sure it is valid. If the certificate is not valid, the browser will display a warning message.

11.3 Handling User Input and Form Validation for Web Security

When handling user input, it is important to consider web security and best practices. There are a number of ways to validate user input, and it is important to choose the most appropriate method for the data being collected.

One common way to validate user input is to use regular expressions. Regular expressions can be used to check that an input value is in the correct format, such as an email address or a credit card number. They can also be used to check that an input value is not in the correct format, such as a phone number or a date.

Another common way to validate user input is to use a whitelist. A whitelist is a list of allowed values, and any input that does not match one of the values on the whitelist is considered invalid. Whitelists can be used to check that an input value is in the correct format, such as a phone number or a date.

Finally, it is also possible to validate user input by using a blacklist. A blacklist is a list of disallowed values, and any input that matches one of the values on the blacklist is considered invalid. Blacklists can be used to check that an input value is not in the correct format, such as an email address or a credit card number.

When choosing a method for validating user input, it is important to consider the type of data being collected and the level of security that is required.

11.4 Protecting Against Cross-Site Scripting (XSS) and SQL Injection for Web Security

One of the most common web security vulnerabilities is cross-site scripting (XSS), which allows an attacker to inject malicious code into a web page that is then executed by the victim's browser. This can be used to steal sensitive information like session cookies, or to hijack the victim's session entirely.

SQL injection is another common web security vulnerability that allows an attacker to execute arbitrary SQL code on the server. This can be used to bypass authentication checks, or to modify data in the database.

To protect against these vulnerabilities, it is important to sanitize all user input before displaying it on the page or inserting it into the database. This includes removing any HTML or SQL code that could be used to exploit the vulnerability.

It is also important to keep all web applications up to date with the latest security patches. This will help to prevent known vulnerabilities from being exploited.

11.5 User Authentication and Authorization for Web Security

User authentication is the process of verifying the identity of a user. This is typically done by prompting the user for a username and password. Once the user enters their credentials, the system verifies that they are correct before allowing the user to access the system.

User authorization is the process of determining what level of access a user has to a system. This is usually based on the user's role within the organization. For example, a user who is an administrator will have different levels of access than a regular user.

Chapter 12: Deploying and Maintaining Websites

12.1 Deploying Websites to a Web Server

In order to deploy a website to a web server, you will need to ensure that you have the necessary permissions and access to the server. You will also need to make sure that the server is configured to host your website. Once you have these things in place, you can use a variety of methods to deploy your website.

One common method is to use a FTP client to connect to the server and upload your website files. Another method is to use a web hosting control panel, such as cPanel, to deploy your website.

Once your website is deployed to the server, you will need to ensure that it is accessible to visitors. This can be done by configuring the server to point to your website's files and by setting up DNS records.

12.2 Domain Registration and DNS Configuration for deploying websites

Domain registration is the process of acquiring a domain name from a domain name registrar. A domain name is an identification string that defines a realm of administrative autonomy, authority, or control within the Internet. Domain names are formed by the rules and procedures of the Domain Name System (DNS).

Any person or entity can register a domain name. Domain names are often seen in email addresses and web site URLs. They can also be used as part of a domain name system, which consists of a network of computers that are used to translate domain names into IP addresses.

DNS configuration is the process of setting up DNS servers to resolve domain names into IP addresses. DNS servers are usually provided by domain name registrars, but they can also be set up by ISPs or other organizations.

DNS servers use a variety of algorithms to determine the IP address that corresponds to a given domain name. The most common algorithm is the Domain Name System Resolver, which is a recursive algorithm that starts at the root DNS servers and works its way down the DNS tree until it finds the desired IP address.

DNS servers can also be configured to use other algorithms, such as the Iterative Resolver or the Linear Search Algorithm. DNS configuration is usually done using a text editor, such as BIND or Microsoft Notepad.

12.3 Website Backup and Version Control

When it comes to website backup and version control, there are a few key things to keep in mind. First, it is important to have a regular backup schedule in place. This will ensure that you always have a recent copy of your website in case something goes wrong. Secondly, it is also important to keep track of all the changes that are made to your website. This can be done using a version control system such as Git. This will allow you to easily revert back to previous versions of your website if necessary.

12.4 Monitoring and Performance Tracking of websites

Monitoring and performance tracking of websites is a process of continuously monitoring a website's performance and availability, and then using that data to identify and diagnose any potential problems. This process can be manual or automated, but either way, it is important to have a plan in place to ensure that website performance is monitored on a regular basis.

There are a number of different metrics that can be tracked when monitoring website performance, including page load times, number of errors, uptime, and more. The most important metric will vary depending on the specific needs of the website, but in general, it is important to track as many different metrics as possible to get a complete picture of the website's health.

There are a number of tools available to help with monitoring and performance tracking of websites. Some of these tools are open source and free to use, while others are commercial products that come with a subscription fee. No matter which type of tool you use, the important thing is to make sure that it meets your specific needs and that you are comfortable using it.

Once you have chosen a tool, the next step is to set up monitoring for your website. This usually involves creating a schedule of when to check the website's performance and configuring the tool to send alerts if there are any problems. Depending on the size and complexity of the website, this process can be fairly simple or quite involved.

Once monitoring is set up, it is important to track the data and look for trends over time. This data can be used to identify potential problems early on and take corrective action to prevent them from becoming bigger issues. Additionally, this data can be used to benchmark the website's performance over time and ensure that it is meeting the needs of its users.

12.5 Continuous Learning and Professional Development in Deploying and Maintaining Websites

Continuous learning and professional development are essential for deploying and maintaining websites. Keeping up with new technologies and trends is crucial for keeping websites up-to-date and secure. In addition, website administrators need to be able to troubleshoot problems and fix errors quickly.

Continuous learning can be achieved through various means, such as attending conferences and workshops, reading trade publications, and taking online courses. Professional development opportunities can also be found through networking and mentorship programs.

Website administrators should always be prepared to learn new skills and technologies. By staying current with the latest trends, they can ensure that their websites are always up-to-date and running smoothly.